DATE DUE			

PADDLE WHEELERS

Robert Shipley/Fred Addis

Great Lakes Album Series

Vanwell Publishing Limited
St. Catharines, Ontario

Canadian Cataloguing in Publication Data
Shipley, Robert, 1948-
    Paddle Wheelers

(Great Lakes album series)
1st Canadian ed.
ISBN 0-920277-61-6

1. Paddle steamers - Great Lakes - History -
Pictorial works. I. Addis, Fred A. (Fred Arthur),
1952-   . II. Title. III. Series

HE566.P3S48 1990   386'.22436'0977   C90-094889-2

Design: Susan Nicholson

Cover: The Chicora enjoyed one of the longest and most colourful careers of any paddle wheeler ever
to sail the Great Lakes. Built in England as a Confederate blockade runner during the American Civil War,
it ended its days as a barge in Kingston, Ontario, on the eve of World War Two. *Marine Museum of Upper Canada, Toronto.*

CONTENTS

Frontier

Large steam driven wheels on either side of the hull propelled the vessel by pushing blades or *paddles* against the water. They gave the name paddle wheeler to several generations of fascinating ships that dominated the Great Lakes. The top part of the paddle wheels were generally hidden from view by a housing, while the bottom portion was usually below the water. Only when a picture captured a vessel out of the water can we glimpse the characteristic machinery. Here the *Frontier* is seen in the Muir Brothers Dry Dock in Port Dalhousie, Ontario, around 1912. The *Frontier* had a long career under several names (see pg. 30).

HISTORY OF PADDLE WHEELERS

Early experiments in France in the 1780s led to the successful use of steam power for the propulsion of ships. The first operational steam driven vessels appeared in Scotland in 1801 and later in America in 1807. The Canadian steam paddle wheeler *Frontenac*, built at Ernestown on the Bay of Quinte, Ontario, and the *Walk-in-the Water* built at Buffalo, New York, marked the introduction of steam power on the Great Lakes in 1816.

Steamboats were initially sailing ships modified for steam propulsion with the addition of paddle wheels at the sides. The tremendous weight of these early cast-iron engines challenged ship builders in their attempt to develop stable vessels. Numerous catastrophes led to the regulation of steam engines. Regular inspection of boilers and machinery, hull designs better suited to the heavy engines and machinery, and the licensing of steam engineers propelled the steam engine into dominance on the lakes by the 1850s.

Side-mounted paddle wheels were favoured on the largely protected waters of the Great Lakes. Being very manoeuvrable and having a shallow draught, they carried tons of cargo and hundreds of passengers to places previously inaccessible. Stern wheelers, typical of the Mississippi, Yukon and other rivers, never enjoyed widespread popularity on the Great Lakes.

Great Lakes ship builders favoured vertical beam or so-called walking beam engines (see pg. 20). These engines, which placed tons of cast iron above the ship's centre of gravity, made paddle wheelers extremely unstable in the heavy seas of the open ocean, but were less of a problem on the lakes. Large waves increased the possibility of one paddle wheel being out of the water while the other was in. This produced stresses on brittle cast-iron parts, which resulted in accidents, delays and costly repairs.

Paddle wheelers opened many areas of the Great Lakes to settlement and economic development. After the advent of railways, these ships were then used to connect railway terminus ports.

Walk-In-The-Water

The name *Walk-In-The-Water* is a direct translation of the name by which the local native people knew this novel craft. We do not know exactly what it looked like when it was built in Buffalo, New York, around 1816, but from old paintings we can assume that the boiler and engine were introduced into a conventional schooner hull and the paddle wheels attached to the sides. Along with the *Frontenac*, built near Kingston, Ontario, about the same time, *Walk-In-The-Water* initiated the age of steam on the Great Lakes. Its career was relatively short, as it was wrecked near Buffalo a few years after being launched.

Buffalo and Erie County Historical Society

Chief Justice Robinson

Named for one of Upper Canada's ruling elite, this handsome early steamer was built by the Niagara Harbour and Dock Company in Niagara-on-the-Lake, Ontario, in 1842. The *Robinson* had a curious ram bow which was said to be designed to break ice. Lake Ontario, where it operated until being scrapped in 1857, seldom froze except along the shoreline and in harbours. *Chief Justice Robinson* could push into this ice sheet and discharge passengers who would then walk ashore over the frozen bridge.

Ontario

Two steamers, both with the name *Ontario*, although built only a generation apart, show the rapid development of marine technology on the lakes. The first was laid down in Sackets Harbour, New York, at the very beginning of the steam era in 1816. It had the traditional schooner hull, sail rigging and low cabin. The later *Ontario* was built in Clayton, New York, in 1847. It had the long sleek steamer hull reinforced by arch trusses, the high forward wheelhouse and the extra two cabin decks running almost the full length of the vessel. The upper decks of such steamers were not an integral part of the vessel's structure. When one of these ships sank, as the *Ontario* did near Quebec City in 1883, the cabins often broke free of the submerging hull and floated. On such occasions the phenomenon saved many lives.

Charles Townsend

The *Charles Townsend* was built by Carrick & Bidwell of Buffalo, New York, in 1834. From this illustration we can see the traditional wooden ship lines with the forepeak still in use. The extensions of deck to the sides to line up with the paddle boxes are supported on struts in a rather makeshift fashion. As well, the ship still carries two masts fitted with loose-footed sails and a substantial jib-boom, indicating less-than-total confidence in the steam power plant.

THE COMING OF STEAM

With the successful introduction of steam power for ship propulsion, demand for this new technology led to several developments. Raising steam pressure in riveted iron boilers often resulted in explosions, ruining both machinery and boat. Double action and compound steam engines were invented to make use of both high pressure steam injected into the cylinder and low pressure steam exhausted and redirected into a larger low pressure cylinder. These types of engine were twice as efficient as their forerunners and much safer.

To increase the power of steam engines, single cylinders reached a size of over a metre (four feet) in diameter. Pistons would travel, or have a stroke, of nearly one and half metres (five feet). Large crank mechanisms would convert the up-and-down motion of the piston to a rotary motion. Paddle wheels, on the outward end of a main shaft, were propelled by the crank mechanisms connected to the piston.

Later steam engines featured multiple smaller cylinders doing the work of a large single cylinder. The injection of expanding gases and the use of super-heated steam provided even more power.

By 1900 steam engines could produce up to 20,000 horsepower. Initially wood was used to fuel their boilers, however coal later became the common fuel. As the movement of bulk raw cargoes became more important, paddle wheelers began to find it hard to compete. The loss of cubic carrying capacity, which resulted from the large spaces required for engine, fuel bunkers and paddle wheel machinery, coupled with the relative thermal inefficiency of steam power, advances in diesel engine technology and screw propulsion, all spelled the end for steam paddle wheelers.

Nevertheless, they enjoyed a longer period of popularity on the Great Lakes than almost anywhere else in the world.

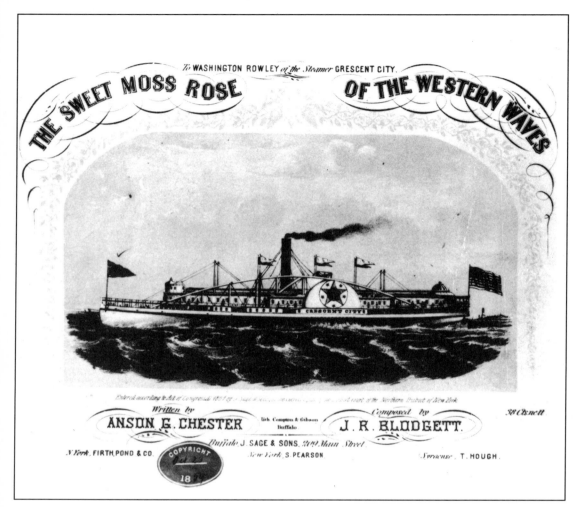

Crescent City

The *Crescent City* was built in Buffalo in 1853 for the New York Central Railway. Before the rail network extended around the Great Lakes and to the west, passengers went as far as Buffalo by train and continued their trip toward the frontier in fast handsome steamers like the one seen here. But this picture is neither an advertisement nor even intended as an accurate portrait of the vessel. This is the cover from a piece of sheet music. It was published only a year after the ship was launched and is dedicated to the captain or some other crewmen of the *Crescent City*.

Buffalo and Erie County Historical Society

THE CLEVELAND LINE STEAMERS.

NORTHWEST | R. N. RICE

Capt. D. A. McLACHLAN. | Capt. WILLIAM McKAY.

Leave the M. C. R. R. wharf, Detroit, daily, at 9 P. M.

SUNDAYS EXCEPTED.

Arrive in Cleveland at 5 A. M.

CONNECTING WITH MORNING TRAINS TO ALL POINTS EAST AND SOUTH.

1877

THROUGH TICKETS TO PRINCIPAL POINTS FOR SALE ON BOARD

AND AT THE

Company's Office, Foot of Shelby Street.

AGENTS ON TRAINS AND AT DEPOTS TO RECEIVE BAGGAGE

Cleveland Line Steamers

This poster advertises two vessels that ran a daily service between Cleveland and Detroit and allowed passengers to make convenient rail connections. It was a very busy and sometimes dangerous route. In 1868, when the steamer *Morning Star* collided with the sailing vessel *Courtlandt*, the *R. N. Rice* was one of the ships that helped to rescue survivors. Both of the stricken ships sank.

Buffalo and Erie County Historical Society

Planet

One of the early generation of Lake Michigan steamers, the *Planet*, is seen in this picture at the Rush Street Wharf in Chicago. It was built in 1855 at Newport, Michigan, and was in service until 1867. At 78 metres (257 feet) in length and almost 10 metres (32 feet) in the beam, the *Planet* was a large vessel in its day.

DEVELOPMENT

Paddles at first were fixed directly to the large circular paddle wheel frames. The paddles pushed down on the water as they entered and backwards as the wheel rotated. To correct the energy lost in the downward motion, paddles were feathered to allow entry at right angles and convert all the energy to the backward motion, which in turn propelled the ship forward.

Side-lever engines and later inclined acting engines increased the stability of paddle wheelers. The side-lever engine placed the heavy beam deep in the hull with connecting rods reaching up to drive the main shaft. The inclined acting engine featured as many as three cylinders acting at an inclined angle to the ship's hull. Both these engines provided greater stability than the high vertical beam engines.

Beech, birch and maple hardwoods provided the fuel for early steam-driven paddle wheelers (see pg. 18). In 1871, eight Calvin and Company steamers burned 23,600 cords of wood, costing more than $56,000 or 41 percent of the company's gross earning for the year.

Engine improvements over the years brought coal consumption down from 1,600 pounds, to produce 50 horsepower for one hour, to around 75 pounds.

St. Catharines Historical Museum

Chicora

After arriving in the Great Lakes from her exciting blockade-running days during the American Civil War, the *Chicora* had two more careers (see cover). In 1868 she was cut in two at Quebec City, floated through the St. Lawrence River and Welland Canal and rebuilt at Buffalo. At 67 metres (221 feet) *Chicora* was too long to fit in the canal locks of the era. She plied the waters of the Upper Lakes between Collingwood and Thunder Bay, Ontario, until 1877 (see pg. 40). It was during that period that this picture was taken in Killarney, Ontario, on the north shore of Georgian Bay. *Chicora* was carrying the Governor General, Lord Dufferin, on a viceregal tour.

Ontario Hydro Archives

Chicora

In 1877 the *Chicora* was again cut in half at Buffalo and taken down the Welland Canal and rejoined at the Muir Brothers Dry Dock in Port Dalhousie, Ontario. It spent the last years of its life as a day steamer running between Toronto and Niagara and finally as a work boat. *Chicora* is pictured here at Queenston, Ontario, in 1903, her decks lined by some of the many passengers who admired her over the years.

Arrow

A number of characteristic features of the classic paddle wheeler can be seen in this very early picture of the American steamer *Arrow*. A conical basket on top of the tall smokestack was designed to catch embers that might have drifted astern and caused fires. The large half-rounded boxes that enclosed the paddles provided a place to display the vessel's name as well as distinctive decorations. The fancy octagonal gazebo wheelhouse was standard for much of the nineteenth century. The cordwood piled on the wharf provided fuel for such a steamer.

Manitoba

The 53-metre (173 foot) passenger steamer *Manitoba* was one of two vessels built at Port Robinson, Ontario, on the Welland Canal, in 1871. Its vertical beam engine had a piston which measured 114 centimetres (45 inches) in diameter with a 2.5-metre (100 inch) stroke. Built for J. H. W. Beatty of Sarnia, Ontario, the *Manitoba*'s career under various names, spanned more than thirty years (see pg. 40).

Public Archives of Ontario

Public Archives of Ontario

Carmona

In 1888 the *Manitoba* was sold to the Northwest Trading Company of Sarnia and renamed *Carmona*. It saw service on Lakes Huron and Ontario. In 1900, under new ownership again, the *Carmona* was lengthened by 15 metres (48 feet) at Collingwood and renamed *Pittsburgh*. Her career on the Detroit River was shortlived, however. The *Pittsburgh* burned to the waterline in 1903.

CLEVELAND & GEORGIAN BAY ROUTE

PITTSBURG

Algoma

National Archives of Canada

The side-wheeler *Algoma* built at Niagara-on-the-Lake in 1839, featured a double vertical beam engine. This allowed the paddle wheels to be operated independently for greater manoeuvrability. Following a fire in 1863 the ship was sold to an American interest and renamed *Racine* operating between Detroit and Lake Michigan ports. Returned to Canada and renamed *Algoma*, it pioneered service between Collingwood and the Canadian Lakehead. In 1881 fire reduced the *Algoma* to a hulk (see pg. 40).

National Archives of Canada

Caspian

Built in Scotland in 1846 as the *Passport*, this steamer was taken apart, transported to Kingston, Ontario, and reassembled. In 1847, it grounded in the St. Lawrence River. When an engineer forgot to shut off a steam intake valve, live steam sprayed on deck. Two people went overboard and were drowned. Forty-four people were severely scalded, thirteen of whom died from their burns. Renamed *Caspian* in 1875, this ship operated until reduced to a tow barge in 1921. The *Caspian* is shown with a typical assortment of cargo waiting to be loaded at Montreal for the return trip to Kingston and Toronto.

Ontario Hydro Archives

St. Lawrence

Famous for her searchlight cruises through the Thousand Islands, the *St. Lawrence* was built at Clayton, New York, in 1884. Her paddle boxes displayed the American eagle on a Thousand Islands background. In 1913 this vessel was acquired by the Canada Steamship Lines. It was scuttled in Lake Ontario in 1924.

EXCURSION BOATS

The development of large population centres around the lakes along with increased leisure time created a market for excursions. Lake shipping companies vied with their competitors for the recreation dollar. Expensive, purpose-built paddle wheelers were designed to accommodate as many as six thousand passengers. Popular excursion routes were the Thousand Islands, Toronto to Niagara, Lake Erie, the Detroit and St. Clair Rivers and Lake Michigan.

The excursion steamers substituted enclosed passenger accommodation space for open promenade decks. Getting there was half the fun, and weekend revellers lined the decks of the smallest to the largest steamers. Amusement parks such as Bob-Lo Island in the Detroit River and Crystal Beach on Lake Erie operated excursion steamers for their patrons.

With the coming of railways and bulk carrying ships, the lives of many paddle wheelers were prolonged by operating in the excursion trade. This however was relatively short-lived, as most disappeared by the 1940s with the advent of private automobiles.

Buffalo and Erie County Historical Society

Spartan

The steamer *Spartan* was laid down in 1864 in the William Gilbert Shipyard in Montreal. It was built for the Royal Mail Line to operate between Montreal and Toronto. *Spartan* had a checkered career. In September 1871 it ran aground on Pigeon Island in the east end of Lake Ontario while en route from Oswego, New York, to Kingston, Ontario. There were several explanations for why the light on the island was out, but fortunately no lives were lost. In 1885 it was wrecked again while on charter in Lake Superior. It was salvaged and returned to the Toronto-Montreal route. Rebuilt and renamed *Belleville* in 1905, it served until being dismantled in 1924.

Illinois

Buffalo and Erie County Historical Society

The *Illinois* was built by E. S. Goodsell of Detroit in 1853 and, as this patriotically decorated sheet music cover indicates, it was the first vessel to go through the newly completed Sault Canal in 1855. The opening up of Lake Superior not only expanded waterborne trade and facilitated the settling of the west, but also increased the scope of pleasure travel. Such events were celebrated in music, part of the popular culture of the day.

Buffalo and Erie County Historical Society

Corona

One of the most popular excursion routes on the Great Lakes carried people from the industrial pressures of nineteenth century Buffalo a short distance across Lake Erie to a relatively pristine string of beaches on the Canadian shore. A number of the beach operators ran their own boats to bring customers from the city. The *Corona*, not to be confused with the larger Canadian registered *Corona* (see next page), was owned by the Woodlawn Beach Company. The profile of a horse mounted on the walking beam, where it would have rocked back and forth as the engine worked, is indicative of the intended playful mood of excursions.

National Archives of Canada

Corona

Launched at Bertram Iron Works of Toronto, Ontario, in 1896, the *Corona* ran between its home port and the Niagara River for most of its career. It was scrapped in 1937. Each summer there was a militia camp held at Niagara-on-the-Lake, Ontario, which drew weekend warriors from across the province. Here we see soldiers as well as holiday makers disembarking from the *Corona.* Fresh Niagara fruit is waiting to be loaded for the return trip to the markets of Toronto.

Argyle

The *Argyle* had three incarnations. It was built as the Empress of India in 1886 in the Bay of Quinte area and spent a number of years in and around the Welland Canal. Returning to Eastern Ontario, it was renamed *Argyle* when it joined the Hepburn Line of Picton. The little girl in the picture is probably Hilda Hepburn, daughter of the owner. About 1912 it was renamed again, becoming the *Frontier* (see pg. 4). Under that title it sank in the Detroit River in 1916. *Argyle* plied the passenger and package freight trade for over forty years. During that time it not only changed names, but underwent at least four major refits, including being lengthened by 4.5 metres (15 feet) and deepened to 3.4 metres (11 feet) in 1899.

St. Catharines Historical Museum

Pennsylvania

The Erie and Buffalo Line steamer, *Pennsylvania*, was a regular at several Lake Erie ports. This ship was later placed in the excursion trade. In 1906 it made the first Sunday sailing from Port Colborne, Ontario, following the repeal of Sabbath Day bylaws on the Welland Canal.

Union

Before a permanent bridge was built between Buffalo, New York, and Fort Erie, Ontario, steamers provided a necessary transportation link across the Niagara River. With horse-drawn buggies on the foredeck and passengers lining the rails aft, the *Union* bucks the current as it approaches the Canadian side. Built in 1864, this venerable side-wheeler was first used on the St. Lawrence River. It sank at its dock in Fort Erie and was abandoned in 1902.

Pearl

Buffalo and Erie County Historical Society

When built at Detroit in 1875, the *Pearl* was considered a large lake steamer at 56 metres (185 feet). Twin arch trusses running along the length of the hull provided stiffening for the wooden hull against the weight of the steam machinery. The *Pearl* was operated by the Crystal Beach Steamboat and Ferry Company until 1906. Larger vessels operated on this run until 1956.

Garden City

The steamer *Garden City* took its name from the community of St. Catharines, Ontario, centre of the Niagara fruit belt. Nearby Port Dalhousie, northern terminus of the Welland Canal, was a popular day-trip destination for the populace of Toronto. The *Garden City* made daily crossings from Toronto from 1892 to 1917. It is seen here about 1910, approaching a wharf in St. Catharines some three kilometres up the Welland Canal.   *St. Catharines Historical Museum*

Cibola

The sleek side-wheeler *Cibola* is seen
coming alongside the wharf at Niagara-
on-the-Lake, Ontario. It was built in 1888
at Deseronto, Ontario, using steel plates
prefabricated in Scotland. *Cibola* operated
on the run between Toronto and Niagara
River ports until an untimely destruction
by fire at Lewiston, New York, in 1895.

Buffalo and Erie County Historical Society

Chippewa

The largest of the steamers on the Niagara run out of Toronto was the stately *Chippewa*. It measures 94 metres (300 feet) in length and with its paddle boxes was almost 30 metres (96 feet) in the beam. As many as two thousand passengers could make the trip upriver to Queenston, Ontario, where a railway connection took them to Niagara Falls. The *Chippewa* was constructed at Hamilton, Ontario, in 1893 and operated until 1939. Like many of the large Lake Erie passenger liners of the same era, it was designed by Frank Kirby of Detroit.

National Archives of Canada

Corsican

This twin-stacked paddle wheeler was built at Montreal in 1870. It is shown shooting the Long Sault Rapids in the St. Lawrence River on its regular run between Toronto and Montreal. The ornate decorative paddle boxes were typical of Victorian era side-wheelers. The iron-hulled *Corsican* burned in Toronto in 1907. Its hull was converted to a barge and renamed *Picton*.

New York

Built for the Thousand Islands excursion service as the *Shrewsbury* in 1896, the *New York* was sold to the Cedar Point Resort Company in Ohio. Its new owners employed it in carrying vacationers from the mainland at Sandusky, Ohio, to their amusement park. Proving too expensive to operate compared with its competition, the *New York* was scrapped in 1908.

OVERNIGHTERS

Prior to the popularity of the private automobile, passenger services linking major lake ports enjoyed widespread use. Services linking Montreal, Kingston and Toronto; Buffalo, Cleveland and Detroit; as well as Lake Michigan ports employed paddle wheelers until the 1950s.

The *City of Buffalo*, known popularly as the Honeymoon Special, carried passengers overnight from Cleveland to Buffalo. The newlyweds would then proceed overland to Niagara Falls. In an era of fine china, silver service, linen napkins, uniformed waiters and polished brass, competing lines upgraded their ships until the largest reached over 150 metres (500 feet) in length and carried five thousand passengers.

The *City of Cleveland* boasted 342 staterooms for overnight accommodation and included an automatic sprinkler system for fire protection. The advertised maximum speed of the ship, under favourable conditions, was not less than 40 kilometres (25 miles) per hour.

"Chicora"   "Algoma"   "Manitoba"   "J. B. Ol

Marine Museum of the Great Lakes at Kingston

Steamers at Thunder Bay

This picture, probably dating from the 1870s, shows three well known paddle wheelers together in the Lake Superior port of Thunder Bay (Port Arthur, Ontario). From left to right they are *Chicora*, *Algoma* and *Manitoba* (see pp. 16, 17, 19 and 22). At the time, all carried both passengers and freight to the Lakehead. The stern view of the *Algoma* shows the extreme beam of a typical side-wheeler's hull and the extra width needed to enclose the paddles.

Buffalo and Erie County Historical Society

State of Ohio

The Detroit and Cleveland Company's steamer *State of Ohio* is shown squaring away to mid-channel in the Cuyahoga River at Cleveland, Ohio, shortly after being placed in the Cleveland and Buffalo service in 1909. The *State of Ohio* made day trips, up one day and down the next, stopping at Erie, Pennsylvania, in both directions. Summer moonlight cruises from each of the terminal cities were always popular.

Buffalo and Erie County Historical Society

State of New York

Launched as the *City of Mackinac* in 1883, this steamer originally sailed for the Detroit and Cleveland Company's Coast Line from Detroit to Mackinac Island and St. Ignace with stops in between. Replaced by larger steamers, it was moved to establish the Cleveland-to-Buffalo night route and renamed *State of New York*. It was again succeeded by larger steamers and rerouted to establish a new service between Cleveland and Toledo, Ohio, followed by yet another reassignment to a new route between Detroit and Saginaw, Michigan. After a fire in 1932, the remains of this ship served as a floating clubhouse for the Columbia Yacht Club in Chicago.

Sheboygan

The twin-stack, arch-trussed, vertical beam paddle wheeler *Sheboygan* was considered to be the finest ship of its type in its day. The relaxed atmosphere on the after deck harkens back to a time when the luxury of lake passenger travel was the preferred way to travel. The *Sheboygan* was built in 1869 and burned as a hulk in 1914. Notice the double chime steam whistle immediately astern of the walking beam between the twin stacks.

Buffalo and Erie County Historical Society

City of Erie

The 100-metre (330 feet) *City of Erie* was built in 1898 by the Detroit Dry Dock Company to take advantage of increased passenger demand on the Cleveland-to-Buffalo route. This steamer operated until the late 1930s when it was laid up. It was sold for scrap in 1941. The *City of Erie* won one of the most famous races ever held on the Great Lakes (see pg. 50).

Buffalo and Erie County Historical Society

City of St. Ignace

Originally built in 1886 as the *City of Cleveland*, this steamer featured a second berth or gallery deck which doubled its capacity as compared to its forerunners. It also operated on the cross-Lake Erie service between Erie, Pennsylvania, and Port Dover, Ontario, as the *Keystone*, before being laid up after a fire in 1932. As the *St. Ignace*, this steamer is shown on the Cleveland, Ohio, to Port Stanley, Ontario, run prior to 1929.

Western States

The D&C liners *Western States* and *Eastern States* were employed on the Detroit, Mackinac and Chicago division. The 110-metre (360 foot) side-wheeler was launched in Detroit in 1902. In 1955, the *Western States* was sold for use as a "flotel." This scheme however failed, and the ship was broken up for scrap in 1959.   *Great Lakes Historical Society, Vermilion, Ohio*

St. Joseph, 18 94.
6L,

Institute for Great Lakes Research, Bowling Green State University

City of Chicago

The Graham and Morton Line steamer *City of Chicago* was one of four steel-hulled paddle wheelers operated by this company to important shipping points and resorts along the Lake Michigan shore. The *City of Chicago* regularly sailed to St. Joseph, Michigan, and in the fall would be seen entering the port of Chicago, Illinois, loaded to the gunwales with thousands of baskets of peaches and other fruit. This steamer was lengthened twice in its career. After being reduced to a barge, it sank in Green Bay in 1942.

Frank E. Kirby

Designed by and named for the noted naval architect Frank E. Kirby, this side-wheeler was called the Flyer of the Lakes, because of its exceptional speed. Among the other Kirby-designed ships were the palatial floating hotel *City of Cleveland* for the Detroit and Cleveland Navigation Company and the *Chippewa* for the Niagara Navigation Company. He also designed Hudson River steamers. The *Frank E. Kirby*, renamed *Dover*, plied between Port Dover, Ontario, and Erie, Pennsylvania, until a fire ended its career in 1929.

THE GRAND SALON

The golden age of Great Lakes luxury liners spanned the first half of the twentieth century. Between 1908 when the *City of Cleveland* was launched at Wyandotte, Michigan, and 1923 when the *Greater Buffalo* was built in Lorain, Ohio, over half a dozen enormous passenger vessels joined the freshwater fleet. Most were side-wheelers. They were the largest vessels of this type ever built. They could carry up to 1,500 cabin passengers and as many as 6,000 day passengers. The passengers' automobiles could even be loaded on to the liners to be available for use when they reached their destinations.

Both the Cleveland and Buffalo Line and the Detroit and Cleveland Company relied primarily on the designs of Detroit naval architect Frank E. Kirby. His reputation for

designing palatial floating resorts was well earned. The appointments of these great vessels were breathtaking. Grand stairways led from spacious dining lounges to vaulted salons. Companionways lined with hardwood panelling led the passengers to their large staterooms.

While some of the vessels lasted into the 1950s, the Second World War marked the end of the era. Two of the great liners of the Lake Erie fleet were in fact converted to aircraft carriers during the war to train fighter pilots.

Cars and planes replaced boats and trains both as a means of transportation and as a form of recreation. As people drove or flew to their vacation destinations the Great Lakes cruise ships vanished one by one.

Tashmoo

The White Star Steamship Company side-wheeler *Tashmoo* is best known for having lost a 100-mile race to the steamer *City of Erie* by a mere forty-five seconds in 1901 (see pg. 44). Built at Wyandotte, Michigan, in 1900, this ship normally ran between Detroit and Port Huron, Michigan. *Tashmoo*, named for an Indian prince of the Chippewa tribe, frequently called at Bob-Lo Island in the Detroit River. During a 1936 cruise the ship's hull was ruptured and over one thousand passengers safely evacuated. The *Tashmoo* was scrapped the same year.

Seeandbee

The rather peculiar name, *Seeandbee*, resulted from a contest sponsored by the C&B (Cleveland and Buffalo) Line when they were building a new boat in 1912. The young woman who suggested the play on the company initials received ten dollars and a free ride on the ship. The *Seeandbee* was over 150 metres (500 feet) long and was said to have been the largest paddle wheeler ever built up to that time.

Seeandbee

The dining rooms in vessels designed by Frank Kirby were usually on a lower deck, where greater stability allowed for comfortable eating. In 1921 the *Seeandbee* began postseason cruises to Mackinac, Sault Ste. Marie, and later to Chicago. From 1913 its regular overnight run had been between Cleveland and Buffalo. By the 1930s it was used exclusively as a cruise ship. Sometimes conventions lasting several days were held aboard. Delegates would have convened in lounges like the one shown on the right.

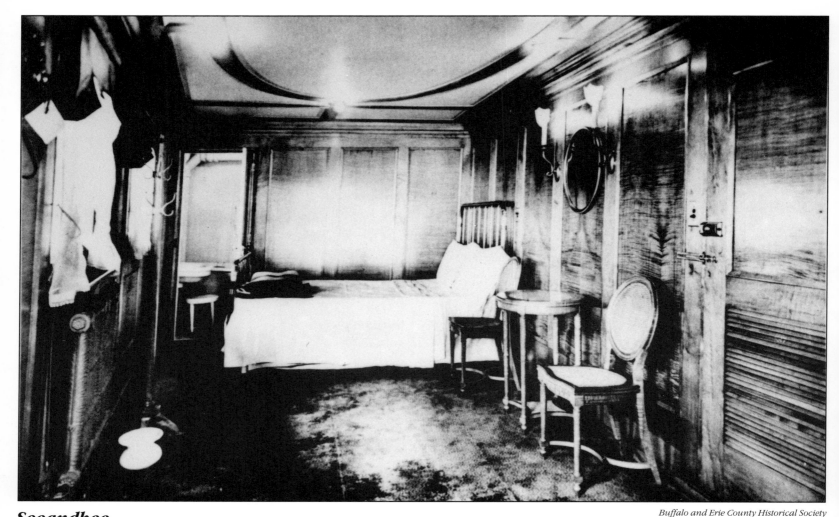

Seeandbee

This was one of the 510 staterooms aboard the *Seeandbee*. Up to 1,500 overnight passengers could be accommodated in all. Cabins were furnished and hospitality provided to a standard matched only by the finest hotels ashore. The wood panelling and art deco furniture and lights were the height of fashion for the period.

Buffalo and Erie County Historical Society

Seeandbee (U.S.S. Wolverine)

It is somewhat ironic that the splendid liner *Seeandbee* ended its days as an aircraft carrier. Drafted into the U.S. Navy at the beginning of the Second World War, it was converted and served to train fighter pilots on the Great Lakes. The *Seeandbee*'s hull was scrapped after the war.

City of Detroit III

Great Lakes Historical Society, Vermilion, Ohio

The Detroit and Cleveland Navigation Company was in direct competition with the Cleveland and Buffalo Line. The D&C liner *City of Detroit III* was commissioned the same year that the C&B brought out the *Seeandbee*. The two liners were fitting rivals, being virtually the same size.

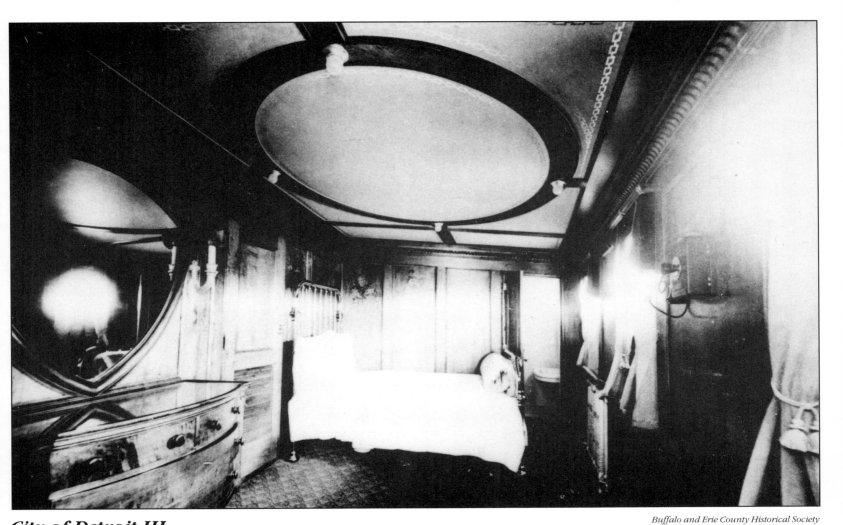

City of Detroit III

Buffalo and Erie County Historical Society

Much of the interior decor, such as this stateroom was saved, when the great ship was broken up in the late 1950s.

Some of the interiors have been preserved at museums.

City of Detroit III

Nowhere was the ornate decoration of the *City of Detroit III* more striking than in the stairways. The painting of mythological figures may have been slightly risqué for the time. Perhaps they amused the honeymooners who rode the ship to Buffalo on their way to Niagara Falls.

City of Detroit III

The magnificent interior of the *City of Detroit III* was designed by Lewis O. Keil.
The showpieces of his work were the galleries which rose through three decks and were crowned with ornate baroque decor.

Greater Buffalo

Institute for Great Lakes Research, Bowling Green State University

The largest of the paddle wheel liners, the 158-metre (519 foot) *Greater Buffalo* ended its days like the *Seeandbee*, in the U.S. Navy. After its last trip as a passenger ship from Detroit to Buffalo in August of 1942, it was rebuilt as an aircraft carrier and renamed the U.S.S. *Sable*.

Greater Detroit

This picture of the *Greater Detroit*, backing away from its slip, captures the excitement of the bon voyage, as we see hundreds of enthusiastic passengers crowding the decks. Several Kirby-designed side-wheelers had bow rudders which, when combined with independent acting paddle wheels, provided great manoeuvrability in the confined waters of many Great Lakes ports and rivers.

Institute for Great Lakes Research, Bowling Green State University

St. Catharines Historical Museum

Toronto

The steam side-wheelers *Toronto* and *Kingston* represent the highest form of development of this type on the Canadian side of the Great Lakes. Operated until 1938 by Canada Steamship Lines, the *Toronto* carried passengers to Prescott, Ontario. There they would be transferred to smaller river steamers for the trip through the rapids to Montreal. The *Toronto* was scrapped in 1947.

Fred Addis

Trillium

The side paddle wheel, steampowered ferry *Trillium*, operated by the Metropolitan Toronto Department of Parks and Property, survives today as the only working reminder of the era of steam paddle wheelers on the Great Lakes.

FURTHER READING

Addis, Fred and John N. Jackson. *The Welland Canals: A Comprehensive Guide*. St. Catharines, Ontario: Lincoln Graphics, 1982.

Baker, A.B. and Tre Tryckare. *The Engine Powered Vessel*. New York: Crescent Books, 1972.

Charlebois, Dr. Peter. *Sternwheelers and Sidewheelers: The Romance of Steamdriven Paddleboats in Canada*. Toronto: NC Press, 1978.

Greenwood, John O. *Namesakes 1900-1909*. Cleveland, Ohio: Freshwater Press Inc., 1986.

Greenwood, John O. *Namesakes 1910-1919*. Cleveland, Ohio: Freshwater Press Inc., 1986.

Greenwood, John O. *Namesakes 1920-1929*. Cleveland, Ohio: Freshwater Press Inc., 1978.

Kemp, Peter, ed. *The Oxford Companion to Ships and the Sea*. London: Oxford University Press, 1976.

Kuttruff, Karl. *Ships of the Great Lakes: A Pictorial History*. Detroit, Michigan: Wayne State University Press, 1976.

Metcalfe, Willis. *Marine Memories*. Picton, Ontario: The Picton Gazette Publishing Co. (1971) Limited, 1975.

Mills, James C. *Our Inland Seas*. Chicago: A. C. McClurg and Company, 1906.

Shipley, Robert J. M. *St. Catharines: A Garden on the Canal*. Burlington, Ontario: Windsor Publications, 1987.

Wilson, Garth S. *Great Lakes Historic Ships Research Project: The Documentation and Analysis of the 19th Century Great Lakes Wooden Hull Design*. Kingston, Ontario: Marine Museum of the Great Lakes, 1989.